# LANGSTON HUGHES
## American Poet

To all children everywhere,

and especially for my great-niece Tiberni Walker.

–A.W.


This book is dedicated to the ones I love.

–C.D.

"When *Susanna Jones Wears Red*" and "The *Negro Speaks of Rivers*"
from "I've Known Rivers" from *The Big Sea* by Langston Hughes.
Copyright © 1940 by Langston Hughes. Copyright renewed 1968 by
Arna Bontemps and George Houston Bass. Reprinted by permission of
Hill and Wang, a division of Farrar, Straus & Giroux, LLC.


Amistad is an imprint of HarperCollins Publishers Inc.

Langston Hughes: American Poet
Text copyright © 1974 by Alice Walker
Author's Note copyright © 2002 by Alice Walker
Illustrations copyright © 2002 by Catherine Deeter
Printed in the U.S.A. All rights reserved.
www.harperchildrens.com

Library of Congress Cataloging-in-Publication Data
Walker, Alice, date.
Langston Hughes: American poet / by Alice Walker ; paintings
by Catherine Deeter.
p.    cm.
Summary: An illustrated biography of the Harlem poet whose works gave
voice to the joy and pain of the black experience in America.
ISBN 0-06-021518-6 – ISBN 0-06-021519-4 (lib. bdg.)
1. Hughes, Langston, 1902–1967–Juvenile literature.
2. Poets, American–20th century–Biography–Juvenile literature.
3. Afro-American poets–Biography–Juvenile literature.  [1. Hughes,
Langston, 1902–1967.  2. Poets, American.  3. Afro-Americans–
Biography.]  I. Deeter, Catherine, ill.  II. Title.
PS3515.IU274 Z9  2002  92-028650
818'.5209  [B]–dc20                                    CIP  AC

Typography by Al Cetta
1  2  3  4  5  6  7  8  9  10
❖

# LANGSTON HUGHES
## American Poet

by Alice Walker
Paintings by Catherine Deeter

HARPERCOLLINSPUBLISHERS

 Amistad

LANGSTON'S FATHER talked and talked, telling them they should stay in Mexico City with him. Langston and his mother and grandmother didn't say anything. They were too tired. They had come by train all the way from Topeka, Kansas, in the United States. It felt good to be resting in a hotel room.

Langston was six years old. He was sleepy and wanted to go to bed. But his grandmother said that would be rude. Langston had not seen his father since he was a baby. Shortly after Langston was born, in 1902, his father had left their home in Joplin, Missouri. Now his mother and father were planning to live together again.

He heard his mother say she would give Mexico City a try.

His father was glad. He said that America was no place for black people to live, because in America white people owned everything. In Mexico, he said, a black person could own something, too.

Mrs. Hughes nodded in agreement.

Just then there was a loud rumbling. It sounded like thunder. The floor began to tremble under their feet. Langston was frightened, and his grandmother swept him into her arms.

The walls of the hotel began to shake. The pictures on the walls fell down with a crash. Langston heard his mother scream. Huge spiders were scurrying through cracks in the walls.

"Earthquake!" shouted Mr. Hughes, as he and Mrs. Hughes fell to the floor.

But in a moment the rumbling stopped. The spiders ran back toward the shelter of the walls. Langston watched his father hit them with his hat. He began to help chase the spiders, amazed to see how fast they went.

Now that the danger was past, he did not feel afraid. He felt excited. He wondered if the big rumbling noise would come often. As he helped his father pick up the fallen pictures, he smiled.

But his mother was already repacking their bags. She wanted to go home, she said. She was trembling, and her voice sounded strange.

In a few minutes they were back at the train station. Langston's father tried to get them to stay in Mexico. But his mother said she was afraid of earthquakes. In a little while they were headed home to Kansas.

Soon after they returned, Langston went to live with his grandmother, Mary Langston. She lived in Lawrence, Kansas. He could not live with his mother because she moved often, looking for work.

His grandmother was a lovely copper-colored woman, with hair so long she could sit on it. From her Langston had gotten his own copper-brown skin and black curly hair.

She told wonderful stories. Langston's favorite story was a true one. It was about his grandfather, Sheridan Leary.

At one time, his grandmother said, black people in the United States were slaves. White people had stolen them from Africa and forced them to work very hard, without pay. Sheridan Leary thought that owning people was wrong, and that black people had to fight to free themselves. He joined some other men and their leader, John Brown, and they set out to fight for the freedom of black people.

After Langston's grandfather left, his grandmother was all alone. One day a package came. It was his grandfather's shawl, riddled with bullet holes. Sheridan Leary had been killed.

"Your grandfather was fighting for freedom," his grandmother said. "He was a great man."

No matter how sad this story sounded while she was telling it, his grandmother never cried. Langston learned not to cry about most things either.

But when his grandmother was not telling stories, Langston felt lonely. He began to read books. He loved the beautiful language in books, and the exciting lives people lived in books. He began to love books more than he loved most people.

Langston lived with his grandmother until he was twelve years old. Soon after she died, his mother sent for him.

Langston's mother was living in Lincoln, Illinois. Sometimes she could not find a job. Then she and Langston had very little to eat. But when she had money, she stuffed him with fancy candies and delicious cakes. She took him to see movies and plays. They laughed a lot and had a good time.

Langston went to school in Lincoln. At the end of his last year, when he was fourteen, his classmates elected him Class Poet because of a poem he wrote.

He'd stayed up all night writing the poem. When he finished reading it, everyone clapped loudly. It made him feel good to know that people enjoyed something he had written.

The day after he was graduated from school, he and his mother moved to Cleveland, Ohio. Langston went to school at Central High. He wrote poems for the school magazine.

He also read stories. Langston decided he would write stories someday, stories about black people. Stories so true that people would still be reading them after he was dead.

At Central High there were many children whose parents had just come to America. There were Jews, Poles, and Hungarians. From them Langston learned that African Americans were not the only people called bad names. He learned that being called "kike" or "hunky" *hurt*, if you were Jewish or Hungarian, just as much as being called "nigger" did if you were black.

Still, his Polish and Jewish and Hungarian friends could get jobs easily during the summer because they were white. Langston had to look and look for a job. The only jobs he could get were the ones the white boys didn't want.

He became lonely for black people. Sometimes, after school, he would go to a nearby drugstore where many black people went. He loved the soft, gentle speech of the black women, and the deep, kind voices of the men. He was happy when

the children played with him. Their faces were yellow, orange-brown, caramel, red-brown, brown, and black.

The girl he liked best often wore a pretty red dress. She had large brown eyes and skin the color of dark chocolate. Her name was Susanna Jones. Langston wrote this poem for her:

## WHEN SUSANNA JONES WEARS RED

*When Susanna Jones wears red*
*Her face is like an ancient cameo*
*Turned brown by the ages.*

*Come with a blast of trumpets,*
*Jesus!*

*When Susanna Jones wears red*
*A queen from some time-dead Egyptian night*
*Walks once again.*

*Blow trumpets, Jesus!*

*And the beauty of Susanna Jones in red*
*Burns in my heart a love-fire sharp like pain.*

*Sweet silver trumpets,*
*Jesus!*

Langston grew tired of cleaning toilets, scrubbing hallways, and emptying garbage for a few cents a week. He did these jobs after school and on weekends. During the summer he worked as a bellhop, helping people with their luggage and carrying messages in a large hotel.

So he was happy one day to get a letter from his father. Mr. Hughes was coming to Cleveland the next day. He wanted to take Langston to Mexico with him for the summer.

Langston was seventeen years old. He had not seen his father since the day of the earthquake eleven years before. Mr. Hughes was now rich. He owned a cattle ranch in Toluca, Mexico, and buildings in Mexico City.

Langston tried to remember what his father looked like. He asked his mother to tell him everything she could about him. But she did not want to talk about Mr. Hughes. Although Mr. Hughes was wealthy, he did not send her any money to help support Langston. She said it was unfair for him to take Langston away for the summer. She said Langston should stay home and earn money for his next year in school.

Because he was running errands for his mother, Langston missed his father's train. But the next afternoon, on his way to the café where his mother worked, Langston met Mr. Hughes on the street. He was small, with light-brown skin and a neat, curved moustache. He came down the street frowning. When he saw Langston, he still didn't smile.

"Are you Langston?" he asked in a sour voice.

"Are you my father?" asked Langston shyly. He waited for Mr. Hughes to put his arms around him. But his father didn't even say he was happy to see Langston. He just started complaining about Langston's mother. He had seen her waiting on tables in the café. He thought waiting on tables was too low-down a job for someone who had been *his* wife.

"If your mother had stayed with me," he told Langston, frowning harder than ever, "she'd be wearing diamonds."

Langston didn't know what to say. He knew his mother worked as a waitress because she couldn't find a better job. It didn't matter that she'd been to college. Hardly anybody wanted to hire black women, except as maids, waitresses, or cooks.

"Just like niggers," his father said. "They will never be anything in America."

Langston hated the word "nigger," and he knew that what his father said was mean and untrue. Maybe his people weren't rich, but he felt they had done great things. He remembered the stories his grandmother had told him about Sheridan Leary.

He knew that his grandfather Charles Langston had been a politician whose fiery freedom speeches brought tears to his eyes when Langston read them. His grandfather's brother, John Mercer Langston, had been a congressman from Virginia after the slaves were freed. He had also been Minister to Haiti and Dean of the Law School at Howard University.

Langston wanted to shout at his father. But because Mr. Hughes made him angry enough to cry, he turned his face away.

He tried to talk to his mother before he left Cleveland. But she was too upset to listen. When he left her, his throat felt all choked up. He could hardly breathe, he felt so bad.

Langston soon realized a sad fact about his father. Mr. Hughes hated black people. He thought it was their own fault that they were poor.

As their train moved southward, through Arkansas, they watched black people working in the cotton fields. They were laughing among themselves, looking happy, although they were poor.

"Look at the niggers," his father said, staring out at the black people as if he could kill them. He thought that because they were poor, black people had no right to laugh.

Langston disagreed. He knew how hard they worked to make a living, and how cruelly they were often treated. He thought it was brave of them to laugh in spite of everything.

On the ranch in Mexico there was an Indian boy who took care of the horses. His name was Maximiliano.

"Never give an Indian anything," Mr. Hughes warned Langston. "He never appreciates it."

But Langston shared his allowance with Maximiliano, and Maximiliano taught him to ride a horse bareback. They became good friends.

All Langston's father cared about was making money. But he never liked to spend any. He would not even buy decent food. For weeks they ate nothing but beans.

Langston hated the stingy, frowning man his father was. At the end of summer he was glad to go home.

After Langston's graduation from Central High in 1920, he talked about going to college. But Langston's mother didn't have any money to send him.

Again Langston's father invited him to Mexico. And because he needed his father's help to go to college, Langston set off.

But he was sad as he took his seat in the train. He thought of his father and shivered. He wanted never to be cut off from his people the way his father was.

No matter what anybody said about black people, Langston knew he would always love them. To him they were courageous and strong.

He thought of the souls of black people as great rivers—rivers very old and deep; rivers that reached all the way back to Africa.

As the train crossed over the muddy waters of the Mississippi River near St. Louis, Langston wrote this poem:

# THE NEGRO SPEAKS OF RIVERS

*I've known rivers:*
*I've known rivers ancient as the world and older than the flow of*
  *human blood in human veins.*

*My soul has grown deep like the rivers.*

*I bathed in the Euphrates when dawns were young.*
*I built my hut near the Congo and it lulled me to sleep.*
*I looked upon the Nile and raised the pyramids above it.*
*I heard the singing of the Mississippi when Abe Lincoln went down to*
  *New Orleans, and I've seen its muddy bosom turn all golden in the*
  *sunset.*

*I've known rivers:*
*Ancient, dusky rivers.*

*My soul has grown deep like the rivers.*

As soon as he reached Mexico, he sent his poem to a magazine in New York called *The Crisis*. It was printed in June 1921. Langston smiled to himself the whole day after he got the news. It was his first poem to be published after high school. Seeing it in the big-city magazine made him feel grown-up and proud.

Mr. Hughes argued that writing was a waste of time. He wanted Langston to go to college in Switzerland and learn to be an engineer.

But Langston insisted he wanted to be a writer. He wanted to go to Columbia University in New York City. He knew that Columbia was close to Harlem, and that black people lived in Harlem. He felt he would be happy there.

Mr. Hughes was angry, but finally he promised to give Langston the money to study at Columbia. At the end of summer Langston went to New York.

At Columbia all his teachers were white. They never talked about anything that concerned black people. Langston felt like an outsider. He was lonely and bored.

Every night he raced over to Harlem, where people were friendly and he could see plays and go to dances and shows. At the end of the year he wrote his father that he was quitting Columbia to find a job. His letter was never answered.

Langston found that jobs were as hard to get as ever. Sometimes he answered ads in the paper that said "Boy Wanted." But when he arrived, the employer would say, "But we didn't advertise for a *colored* boy!"

This made Langston mad. He thought it was stupid for white people not to hire him just because his skin was black.

Some people, when they have a hard time, stay mad, with their lips poked out. But not Langston. When he felt bad, he sat down and wrote poems until he felt better. Then he went out partying with his friends.

Luckily he was able to sign on as messboy on a ship going to Africa. He had wanted to see Africa ever since his grandmother had told him that it was where black people had come from. His job was to clean up the mess hall, where the sailors ate.

As the ship left New York harbor, Langston threw all his books overboard. He had decided it was wrong to love books more than people. He wanted to live life firsthand, seeing it with his own eyes; not secondhand, through books.

The west coast of Africa was a long, sugar-white beach, with green palm trees swaying above. The African people Langston met were tall and black-skinned. The men were friendly and handsome, the women bright-eyed and shy. They asked many questions about America, and were surprised that Langston considered himself part African. They said he looked like a white man, because his skin was so light a brown.

Langston assured them he was not white. He also told them he was a writer and promised he would write stories about them someday.

When he returned to America, his mother was living in Washington, D.C. There the only work Langston could find was in a hot, steamy laundry. He wrote poems between loads of wash. When he came down with a cold because of the steam and had to stay home for a few days, his boss fired him.

His next job was as busboy at the Wardman Park Hotel. He cleared the dirty dishes from the tables in the dining room. One day he saw the famous poet Vachel Lindsay sitting at one of his tables. Quickly he wrote down three of his poems and put them next to Mr. Lindsay's plate.

The next morning there was a story about Langston's poems in the newspaper. In the story Mr. Lindsay said that he had read Langston's poems and that Langston was a good poet. Men came with cameras to take Langston's picture.

The next summer Langston received forty dollars and a gold medal for several of his poems. Some time later his first book of poems, *The Weary Blues*, was published.

But Langston knew that most black people were too poor to buy his book. So he decided to travel all over the country reading his poetry. When his audiences could afford to pay, they did. Langston was able to make a small amount of money. And he was able to see, face-to-face, the people he wrote for and about.

By the time he was thirty years old, Langston was beginning to make his living by writing. He helped other black people who wanted to write. He gave them encouragement and advice. Sometimes he would pay to have their stories or poems printed in books.

This did not mean that Langston made a lot of money from his writing. He didn't. But he was never stingy with money like his father.

When his father died, Langston went to Mexico for the reading of his will. He did not think Mr. Hughes had left anything for him, and he was right. His father did not leave one penny of his money to Langston, although Langston was his only son. He was stingy to the end.

Every time his mother needed money, she wrote to Langston. She never believed he could write so many books and still be broke. Langston would always send her what money he could, even if he had to borrow it. But he was sorry she never understood.

As he grew older, Langston was able to travel all over the world as a writer. People in Africa, Asia, Europe, and the Caribbean islands had read his stories. By the time he was fifty years old, he had written more than two dozen books. He had written books of poems and stories, novels, plays, children's books, and even history books.

He always wrote truthfully about black people. He showed that they were beautiful, and sometimes ugly, like most people. He showed that they were sometimes happy and sometimes sad—and that they could laugh even when they were feeling blue. He always thought this ability made them special.

When Langston Hughes died in 1967, people all over the world were sad. But they knew Langston did not believe in crying. He would want his friends to be happy they were still alive. He would want them to love and help one another.

At his funeral there was music—jazz and blues. Many of Langston's poems were read. His friends had a chance to meet.

It was sad and happy at the same time. His friends were sad that Langston had gone away but glad that they had known him. They were sad that they would no longer see him walking down the streets of Harlem but happy that his spirit lived in each of them.

Langston Hughes had shown them how good it was to love one another. And this love, like his poems, would live forever—amid the deepest laughter of their own hearts.

# Author's Note

IT WAS DURING MY senior year at Sarah Lawrence College that I met the poet Langston Hughes. My poetry teacher, Muriel Rukeyser, a friend of Langston's, sent my short story "To Hell With Dying" to him to see what he thought. He said he loved it and asked if he could print it in an anthology, *The Best Short Stories by Negro Writers*, that he was at the moment editing. Of course I said yes. Shortly thereafter Langston Hughes invited me to come to Harlem, where one of his plays was being performed. I don't recall the play, but I remember vividly the warmth in his eyes as he took my hand and smiled at me. He said I reminded him of "a young Ruby Dee." I did not know this famous actress at the time, but from the moment he said that, I felt a special bond with her, and I have been moved to witness in her life a generosity to young people similar to Langston's.

Langston Hughes was a very busy man. Always writing, or producing plays, or editing books, or traveling. Yet he found time to write to me from time to time. To my delight he always used bright-green ink! He wrote me once that he was ill with the flu. I bought a bag of oranges and took them to his door. He was beginning to recover and moved slowly about his modest third-story flat. He asked me which of his books I'd most enjoyed reading. I was saddened to reply that I didn't know his books. He reached into a cabinet near his desk and piled my arms high with what appeared to be copies of every book he'd written. I took them back to school in a large string bag and began that very night to read them. I found I liked his poetry, but even more compelling for me was his autobiographical writing, especially *The Big Sea* and *I Wonder as I Wander*. In these books I encountered a spirit very like my own: a spirit that loves people, enjoys variety, hungers for diversity and change. He'd also had a lot of difficulty surviving his childhood. Many writers are reluctant to write about how hard it can sometimes be to understand parents and society and the way the world is organized, but not Langston. Because he wrote so honestly about his struggles with his parents, and the often-puzzling cruelties of other human beings, I felt I could trust him as a writer who still remembered the world of childhood. I wished I had known about him and his books when I was growing up. They would have been a big help to me.

Realizing this, I saw what I must do. From the moment I understood what I had missed, not having Langston's stories of his life to help guide me, I resolved to make it possible for children everywhere to be aware of his existence. And that is why I wrote this book.

There are places in the world that emit so much magnetism, energy, and power that people who visit them call them holy. There are people who have this quality too. Langston was one of them. He was a person who loved unconditionally. He seemed to gaze directly into the heart; gender and race, for instance, were not barriers for him. It was possible to feel this love, like a kind of radiance, all around him. That is why so many people loved him in return. He was accepting of others, patient with them, and capable of finding humor in the most complicated experiences of life. He was also thoughtful and humble. And very, very wise.

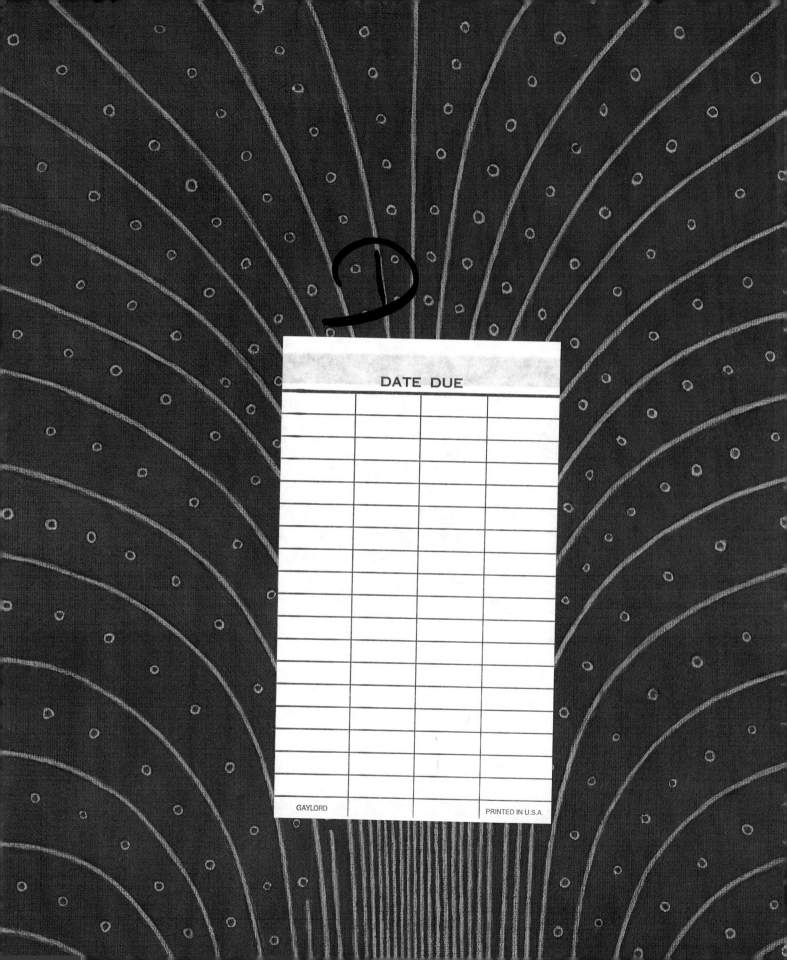